KWJC

TULSA CITY-COUNTY LIBRARY

W9-ANO-030

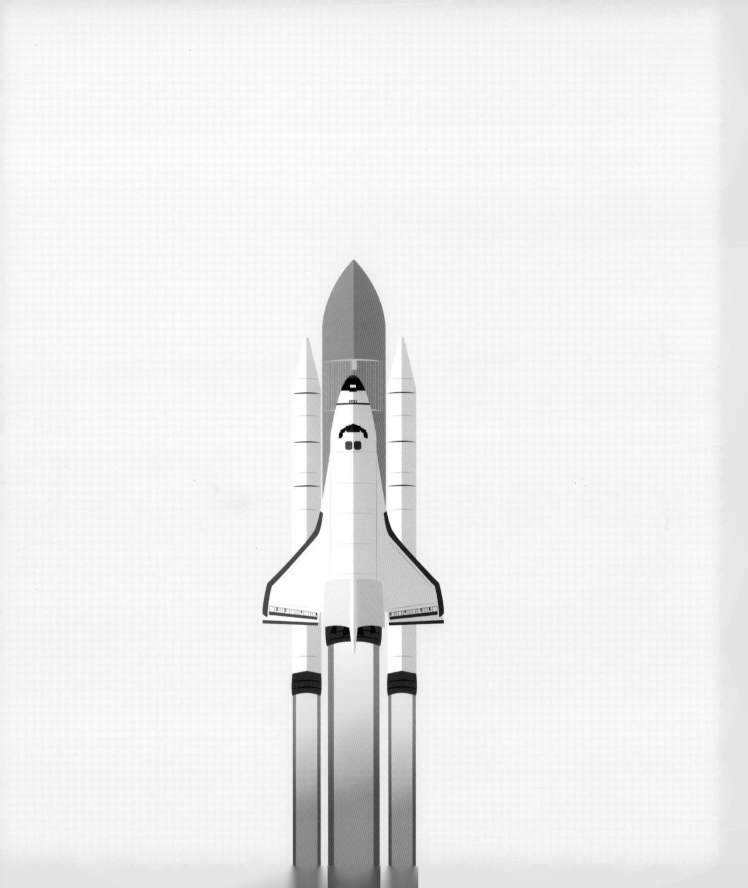

Author:
Alex Woolf studied history at Essex University in England. He is the author of many books for children on science topics, including previous titles in The Science Of series on rocks and minerals and natural disasters.

Series creator:
David Salariya was born in Dundee, Scotland. He has illustrated a wide range of books and has created and designed many new series for publishers in the UK and overseas. David established The Salariya Book Company in 1989. He lives in Brighton, England, with his wife, illustrator Shirley Willis, and their son, Jonathan.

Artists:
Ed Myer, Bryan Beach, Jared Green, Sam Bridges, and Shutterstock.

Editor:
Nick Pierce

PAPER FROM
SUSTAINABLE
FORESTS

© The Salariya Book Company Ltd MMXIX
No part of this publication may be reproduced in whole or in part, or stored in a retrieval system, or transmitted in any form or by any means, electronic, mechanical, photocopying, recording, or otherwise, without written permission of the publisher. For information regarding permission, write to the copyright holder.

Published in Great Britain in 2019 by
The Salariya Book Company Ltd
25 Marlborough Place, Brighton BN1 1UB

Library of Congress Cataloging-in-Publication Data

Names: Woolf, Alex, 1964- author. | Myer, Ed (Illustrator), illustrator. | Beach, Bryan, illustrator.
Title: The science of spacecraft : the cosmic truth about rockets, satellites, and probes / written by Alex Woolf ; [artists, Ed Myer, Bryan Beach].
Description: New York, NY : Franklin Watts, an imprint of Scholastic Inc., 2019. | Series: The science of... | Includes index.
Identifiers: LCCN 2018031801| ISBN 9780531131978 (library binding) | ISBN 9780531133972 (pbk.)
Subjects: LCSH: Space vehicles--Juvenile literature. | Space flight--Juvenile literature. | Astronautics--Juvenile literature. | Outer space--Exploration--Juvenile literature.
Classification: LCC TL793 .W657 2019 | DDC 629.47--dc23

All rights reserved.
Published in 2019 in the United States
by Franklin Watts
An imprint of Scholastic Inc.

Printed and bound in China.
Printed on paper from sustainable sources.
1 2 3 4 5 6 7 8 9 10 R 28 27 26 25 24 23 22 21 20 19

SCHOLASTIC, FRANKLIN WATTS, and associated logos are trademarks and/or registered trademarks of Scholastic Inc.

This book is sold subject to the conditions that it shall not, by way of trade or otherwise, be lent, resold, hired out, or otherwise circulated without the publisher's prior consent in any form or binding or cover other than that in which it is published and without similar condition being imposed on the subsequent purchaser.

The Science of Spacecraft

The Cosmic Truth About Rockets, Satellites, and Probes

written by
Alex Woolf

Franklin Watts®
An Imprint of Scholastic Inc.

Contents

Introduction

Space has been a source of fascination to humans for thousands of years. For virtually all of that time, our only means of understanding the cosmos has been by looking at it from Earth's surface. That changed in the 1940s with the building of the first vehicles capable of resisting Earth's gravity and reaching space. These and later spacecraft have enabled us to journey to the Moon, the planets, and other bodies in orbit around the Sun.

In this book we'll look at the many different kinds of spacecraft in use today, from the artificial satellites that orbit Earth to the probes that explore the furthest reaches of our solar system. We will learn how they are built, how they navigate and communicate, and what operations they perform as they travel through their airless environment.

Yuri Gagarin

In the early 1960s, spacecraft were developed that could carry humans. The first human in space was Soviet air force pilot Yuri Gagarin. On April 12, 1961, he circled Earth once in his spacecraft Vostok 1. Valentina Tereshkova was the first woman in space, in 1963.

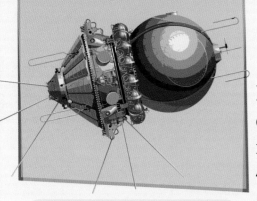

In 1981, the US launched the first reusable spaceplane, the Space Shuttle. These blasted off like rockets and landed like airplanes. Shuttles carried satellites and probes into space and resupplied space stations.

How Did Space Travel Begin?

The first steps on our journey into space were taken in the early 20th century when scientists in the US, Russia, and Germany made important advances in rocket science. In 1949, the US launched the first rocket to reach space. It had two sections or "stages," each with an engine and fuel. When the first stage used up its fuel, it dropped back to Earth. On October 4, 1957, the Soviet Union launched the first artificial satellite, Sputnik, sending it in orbit around Earth. This achievement caused huge excitement and spurred the US, its rival, to even greater efforts. The Space Race had begun.

Sputnik

One Giant Leap

In July 1969, the US won the race to put a human on the Moon. The Apollo 11 spacecraft carried three astronauts, Neil Armstrong, Buzz Aldrin, and Michael Collins, to the Moon. Armstrong became the first person to walk on the Moon's surface.

In 1971, the Soviet Union launched the first space station, Salyut 1, a satellite designed to support human life, enabling people to remain in space for an extended period.

Space Probes

In the 1960s and 1970s, attention turned to the exploration of the planets. Probes (unpiloted spacecraft) were sent on missions to Mercury, Venus, Mars, Saturn, and Jupiter. Launched in 1977, US probes *Voyager 1* and *2* explored the outer solar system, and they're still going today.

Fascinating Fact

After Apollo 11 astronauts Neil Armstrong and Buzz Aldrin returned to the Lunar Module (the lander that carried them from their spacecraft to the lunar surface), they realized the ignition switch was broken. Aldrin jammed his pen into the mechanism to create a makeshift switch, and they were able to take off.

I knew this pen would come in handy!

IGNITION

7

How Does a Rocket Work?

A rocket's thrust pushing it upward must be powerful enough to overcome its own weight (the force of gravity) and the air resistance (drag) pulling it down.

Rockets Are Like Balloons

When you let air out of a balloon, the air goes one way, and the balloon moves in the opposite direction. Rocket engines work in the same way. Exhaust gases from the fuel pouring out of the engine's nozzle at high speed push the rocket forward.

A rocket is a missile, aircraft, or spacecraft that gets its thrust (propulsive power) from a rocket engine. Rockets are the only means humans have developed so far for reaching space. The first rockets were developed by the Chinese in the 13th century. Powered by gunpowder, they were used as explosive weapons in battles and sieges. In 1903, Russian scientist Konstantin Tsiolkovsky first speculated on the possibility of using rockets for spaceflight. American rocket scientist Robert Goddard made the decisive breakthrough with the launch of the first liquid-fueled, steerable rocket in 1926, ushering in the Space Age.

One day we'll send these to space!

Not with me in it!

Rocket Fuel

Most rocket propellant (fuel) is either solid or liquid.

1. Solid-propellant rocket engines are relatively simple, safe, and cheap. However, the thrust cannot be controlled, and the engine, once started, cannot be stopped. They are used in external rocket boosters, assisting the main rocket engine.

2. Liquid propellants are lighter and therefore more efficient, and can provide variable thrust, so are commonly used in the main engine. However, they generate so much heat inside the engine's combustion chamber that they must be cooled by a complex system of pumps.

1.

Combustion chamber

Solid fuel and oxidizer

Payload

2.

Pumps

Liquid fuel

Liquid oxidizer

Payload

Try It Yourself

Make a balloon rocket. Tie one end of a long piece of string to a doorknob. Put the other end through a straw. Pull the string tight and tie it to a chair.

Next, blow up a balloon, but don't tie it. Keeping its end pinched closed, tape the balloon to the straw. Let go, and watch the balloon rocket fly!

Rocket Structure

Modern rockets are very complex and contain about three million parts. However, they all have the same basic structure: a propulsion system (engine, fuel tanks, boosters), a guidance system (computer-based navigation system), and a payload (whatever it's carrying, whether it is people or a satellite).

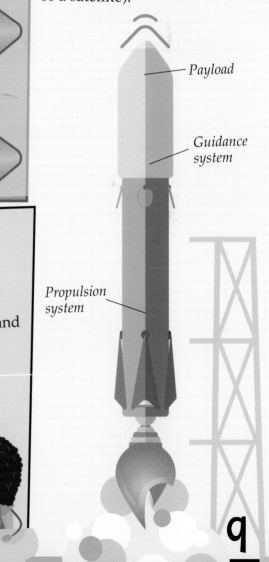

Payload

Guidance system

Propulsion system

Artificial Satellites

Some satellites carry space telescopes, such as the Hubble. These avoid the problems of Earth-based telescopes, such as light pollution and atmospheric distortion.

The Global Positioning System (GPS)

This is a network of 31 satellites that send out regular signals. A GPS receiver such as a cell phone is always within range of at least four of these satellites, and uses them to pinpoint its exact location.

A satellite is a celestial body that orbits a planet. The Moon, for example, is a satellite of Earth. Since the 1950s, Earth has acquired many more satellites— these are artificial (human-made), and they were placed in orbit by rockets. The first, launched in 1957, was Sputnik (see page 6). Since then, around 6,600 satellites have been launched by over 40 countries. More than a thousand are in operation today.

Artificial satellites do many important jobs. They are used for telecommunications (transmitting phone calls and other digital information around the world), navigation (GPS), weather forecasting, astronomical observation, monitoring Earth, and spying on other countries.

There's no way through!

Communication Satellites

These satellites relay radio waves (for TV, phone, or Internet transmissions) from one place on Earth to another. They receive signals from Earth-based transmitters, then relay them to a receiver somewhere else. They overcome the problem that our planet is curved, but radio waves move only in straight lines.

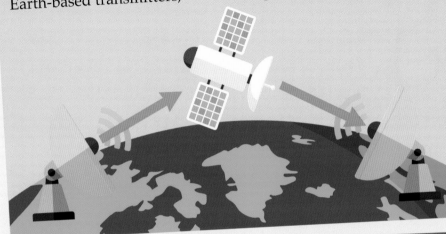

Satellite Orbits

The three most common satellite orbits are:
• Low Earth Orbit (LEO): up to 1,250 miles (2,000 kilometers); includes Earth observation and spy satellites.
• Medium Earth Orbit (MEO): 12,500 miles (20,000 km); includes GPS satellites.
• Geosynchronous Orbit (GEO): 22,500 miles (36,000 km); satellite stays above same point on Earth's surface; includes communications and weather satellites.

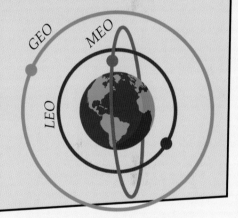

Why It Works

Every satellite has the same basic parts:
• bus—the frame to which all other parts are attached
• power source—most are powered by solar panels
• computer system—to control operations and monitor orientation
• communications—to send and receive data from ground stations
• attitude control—gyroscopes and thrusters to maintain orientation

Earth observation satellites photograph, map, and monitor Earth's surface, keeping scientists updated about developments, such as sea level changes and Arctic ice cap shrinkage.

Bus

Thruster

Computer system

Power source

Communications

Space Probes

Equipment

Space probes carry sophisticated scientific instruments and tools, enabling them to study the celestial bodies they visit. Their cameras take photographs, and their sensors analyze atmosphere, temperature, magnetic field strength, radiation, and chemical composition.

Sensor

Camera

The first space probes were the *Luna* spacecraft (1959–1976), sent to explore the Moon. The *Mariner* probes (1962–1973) were the first to explore Mercury, Venus, and Mars. *Pioneer 10* (launched 1972) completed the first mission to Jupiter.

Since 1959, space agencies have launched many missions beyond Earth's orbit, to explore outer space. Except for the Apollo missions to the Moon (1961–1972), all these missions have been performed by pilotless, robotic spacecraft called space probes. There have been space probe missions to all the planets and several of the moons, asteroids, and comets of the solar system. Some fly by or go into orbit around these bodies; others collide with or land on them. Space probes are a useful means of exploring space because human spaceflight is both dangerous and expensive. Probes don't need to carry food, water, or oxygen, and can withstand conditions that would be fatal to astronauts.

Communication

Space probes are equipped with computers that convert the information they collect into digital signals. A transceiver, or dish antenna, sends these in the form of radio waves back to Earth, where they are picked up by powerful antennas and converted back into pictures and useful information.

Propulsion

All space probes must use rocket engines to escape Earth's gravity. Once in outer space, probes may be propelled by other means such as chemical fuel cells or batteries. Future probes might use solar sails, which are giant reflective sheets. Billions of light particles from the Sun are enough to propel the probe, similar to the way the wind blows the sail of a boat.

Mission control on Earth figures out the location of a probe by measuring the time it takes for signals to be sent and received, and by studying photographs sent back by the probe. Mission control uses this information to help keep the probe on course.

Can You Believe It?

Some probes use the gravity of planets to help them on their way through space. This process, called gravity assist, can save fuel and get them to their destinations faster. A probe can "steal speed" from the planet by flying past it in the same direction the planet is orbiting, or slow down by flying by in the opposite direction.

Space Studies

- Space stations are used to study how living in space affects the human body, in preparation for future crewed missions to Mars or other planets.
- In microgravity, near-perfect crystals can form, which may lead to faster computers and more-efficient medicines.
- In microgravity, flames are slow and steady, making it easier to study combustion, which could lead to advances in furnace design and a reduction in air pollution.

Fire sure burns differently up here!

The space station Mir stayed in space from 1986 to 2001. It was continuously occupied by humans for a record 3,644 days, with one astronaut spending 438 days on the station.

Space Stations

Most human-operated spacecraft spend just a few days in space. Space stations, however, allow astronauts to spend months or even years in orbit around Earth. These structures provide a temporary home for crew members where they can conduct scientific experiments in weightless conditions. Unlike other kinds of spacecraft, space stations do not have major propulsion or landing systems. Instead, other spacecraft ferry people and cargo to and from the space station.

Space Colonies?

In future, space stations might be launched by private companies as "space hotels." They could be used as space ports for expeditions to other planets. They may even one day be home to space colonies —cities in space—growing their own crops and living independently of Earth.

Challenges

Prolonged exposure to weightlessness and higher levels of radiation in space leads to health problems in astronauts, including bone and muscle deterioration and a higher risk of cancer. If humans are to live for long periods in space stations, they may need to be equipped with artificial gravity and radiation shielding.

Fascinating Facts

The International Space Station (ISS):
- travels around Earth at 5 miles (8 km) a second;
- is 358 feet (109 meters) long;
- was built by sixteen countries;
- is the most expensive object ever built, costing over $120 billion;
- is currently the third brightest object in the night sky after the Moon and Venus.

The size of a five-bedroom house and as large as a football field, the ISS is the biggest spacecraft ever built. It was completed in 2011 and is expected to operate until 2028. It is powered by solar energy and has labs for science research.

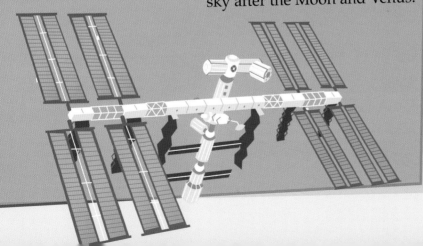

Why use spaceplanes? As single-use machines, rockets are expensive and wasteful. Spaceplanes offer a relatively cheap means of getting into space.

What Is a Spaceplane?

A spaceplane is a vehicle that operates as an aircraft in Earth's atmosphere and as a spacecraft when in space. Spaceplanes typically have wings to give them lift when in Earth's atmosphere. They take off vertically and have powerful rocket engines to reach space. After their spaceflight, they reenter the atmosphere and land without power, like a glider. To date, five spaceplanes have flown: Space Shuttle, Buran, Boeing X-37, North American X-15, and SpaceShipOne. The most successful was Space Shuttle, which operated from 1981 to 2011.

Liftoff

Two minutes after liftoff, at a height of 28 miles (45 km), the Space Shuttle's two solid rocket boosters (SRBs) separated from the fuel tank. The SRBs descended on parachutes and were retrieved. At 70 miles (113 km) up, the external fuel tank, its fuel spent, was jettisoned. The shuttle then fired its engines to achieve orbit.

The Flight

The Space Shuttle flew at around 17,500 miles per hour (28,000 kph), circling Earth once every 92 minutes. Each mission lasted seven or eight days. The cargo bay was big enough to hold a bus. It carried satellites and probes, as well as labs, into space. Astronauts carried out experiments and performed space walks.

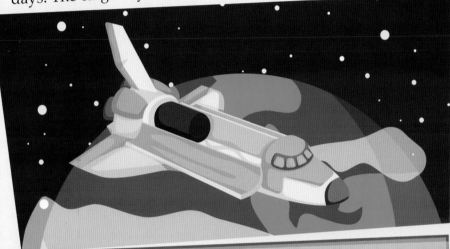

Reentry

Before reentering Earth's atmosphere, the crew slowed the shuttle down and rolled it over so the bottom faced the atmosphere. As it struck the air molecules, the orbiter's base heated up from friction. Its heat-resistant tiles protected it from searing 3,000°F (1,648°C) temperatures.

Why It Works

The Space Shuttle had two SRBs along with a jet engine to launch the vehicle into space. The SRBs were connected to a huge external fuel tank that was attached to the orbiter—the winged craft that carried the crew. The orbiter was 122 feet (37 m) long and had a wingspan of 78 feet (23 m).

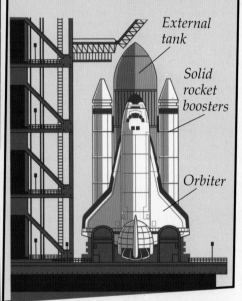

External tank

Solid rocket boosters

Orbiter

The Space Shuttle provided crew rotation for the ISS, performed satellite servicing and repair, and could recover old satellites and return them to Earth.

What Are Landers and Rovers?

Slowing the Descent

Sometimes landers fire rockets to reduce their impact velocity. If the celestial body has an atmosphere, the lander can deploy a parachute to slow itself down as it descends. Landers are fitted with padded legs or airbags for a softer landing.

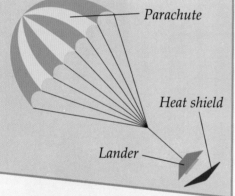

Parachute

Heat shield

Lander

When the lander *Pathfinder* reached Mars on July 4, 1997, it opened its body like the petals of a flower and out rolled *Sojourner*, the first rover to be deployed on another planet.

Space probes can fly through space to visit planets and other celestial bodies, and can even crash into them, but they cannot make a controlled landing on them, much less move across their surface. For that we need two other kinds of space vehicle—landers and rovers. Landers are spacecraft designed to descend slowly and come safely to rest on the surface of a celestial body. They have been used on the Moon, Mars, Venus, and Titan (a moon of Saturn), as well as on asteroids and a comet. Rovers explore a body's surface and take samples. They are usually brought to the surface by a lander. Rovers sent to the Moon and Mars have been highly successful.

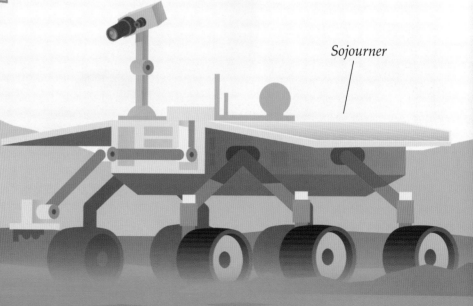

Sojourner

Landing on a Comet

On November 12, 2014, the *Rosetta* probe put the robotic lander *Philae* on comet Churyumov-Gerasimenko. Due to the low gravity, *Philae* had to fire a harpoon at the comet so it could anchor a cable in the surface and pull itself down. The harpoon failed to deploy and *Philae* bounced twice, but still managed to land.

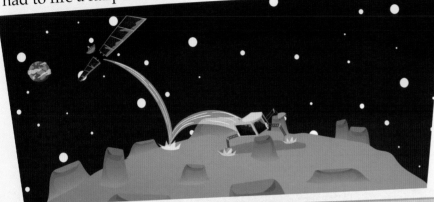

Can You Believe It?

Engineers are researching non-wheeled designs for rovers to explore low-gravity bodies like asteroids and comets, including rovers that walk or roll. One possibility is the "Hedgehog," a cube-shaped rover that can hop and tumble across a surface. If it is stuck in a hole, it can escape by corkscrewing upward.

Intelligent Rovers

Rovers operating on distant bodies cannot be controlled remotely because radio signals take too long for real-time communication. So rovers are equipped with computers that can decide where to go and which samples to retrieve. Human input is still needed, for example, to identify promising targets in the distance.

The rover *Opportunity* reached Mars in January 2004, and was expected to function for three months. Remarkably, it was still active in June 2018. It has traveled over 28 miles (45 km), survived dust storms, and discovered a meteorite.

Before a space walk, astronauts breathe 100 percent oxygen until all the nitrogen has left their bodies, to avoid a sickness called the bends.

How Does a Space Suit Work?

Space Walks

Astronauts exit the spacecraft via an airtight room called an airlock. The exterior of the spacecraft has handrails to help them move from place to place. They attach themselves to the spacecraft with tethers (ropes) to avoid floating away. They tether their tools to their space suits.

Sometimes astronauts must leave their spacecraft to conduct experiments or repair equipment. Space is a very hostile environment for humans, with no air, extreme temperatures, micrometeorites, and harmful radiation. To protect themselves, astronauts wear space suits. A fully equipped space suit provides for all the astronaut's needs, including oxygen, water, temperature control, a communication system, waste disposal, and mobility.

Staying Safe

During extravehicular activities (EVA), astronauts wear a SAFER (Simplified Aid for EVA Rescue) on their backs. SAFER has small jet thrusters, controlled by a joystick, that allow an astronaut to move around in space. If an astronaut became untethered and floated away, SAFER would enable him or her to fly back to the spacecraft.

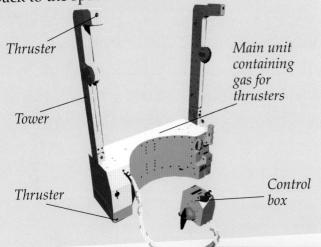

Thruster

Tower

Thruster

Main unit containing gas for thrusters

Control box

Suitports

A future alternative to the airlock may be the suitport, in which the back of the space suit is attached to the outside of a spacecraft. The astronaut climbs inside it and detaches it from the craft. This can prevent harmful space dust from entering the spacecraft and greatly reduce exit and reentry times for EVAs.

In 1965, Alexei Leonov performed the first space walk. It lasted 10 minutes. The record for most space walks is held by Anatoly Solovyev, with 16 EVAs.

Why It Works

Space suits include a backpack called the Portable (or Primary) Life Support System (PLSS). This supplies the astronauts with oxygen and removes the carbon dioxide they exhale, and it supplies electric power to the suit, a ventilating fan and water-cooling system, and communication equipment.

Cleanrooms

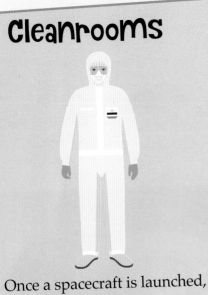

Once a spacecraft is launched, making repairs is very expensive, so great care is taken at the building stage. Spacecraft are built and tested in cleanrooms, where the air is filtered to remove most of the dust and moisture. People working there must wear an all-in-one "bunny suit," plus a face mask and gloves.

There's no air in space, so spacecraft don't need to be streamlined. Satellites that spin are drum-shaped, but most satellites are box-shaped.

How Do You Build a Spacecraft?

Spacecraft are not mass-produced like cars. They are often one-of-a-kind machines, designed and put together by hand to fulfill a particular purpose. Even so, they usually have very similar basic structures. Satellites, for example, are made up of two main sections: the platform, which includes the framework, engine, fuel tank, boosters, and power supply; and the payload, which consists of the instruments the satellite needs to do its work in space, such as cameras and communication systems.

Testing

Once a spacecraft is built, it must be tested. It is placed in a chamber that simulates the deafening noise and violent shaking of a launch. Then the spacecraft is exposed to the freezing and roasting temperatures of space. Its electrical systems are tested inside a powerful magnetic field—another hazard of space.

Future spacecraft could be made from carbon nanotubes, which are ultra-light and 600 times stronger than steel. If filled with hydrogen, these may offer radiation shielding.

Solar Panel Origami

Satellites have to be small enough to fit inside the nose of a rocket. But solar panels are more useful when they're big. Researchers have been inspired by origami to create a folded panel 9 feet (3 m) in diameter that, once in orbit, could unfold to become a solar panel 82 feet (25 m) wide.

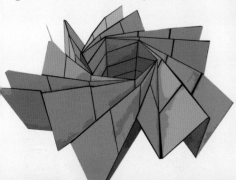

Try It Yourself

Draw a satellite.
1. Start by drawing the platform (a rectangle).
2. Next, add the satellite dish at its base (a dish shape with a long thin antenna in the middle).
3. Then add the solar panels (two large rectangles each containing a grid of horizontal and vertical lines).
4. Finally, color it in.

Space Telescopes

The James Webb Space Telescope, set to launch in 2021, will be the most powerful yet. It will be able to see vast distances, back to the early history of the universe.

Hubble Space Telescope

Hubble offered views in visible, infrared, and ultraviolet light. However, the images sent back to Earth were blurry, because its main mirror had been ground to the wrong shape. Astronauts were sent up to insert new mirrors to correct the fault, like giving it a pair of eyeglasses. Soon, Hubble was beaming amazingly clear views.

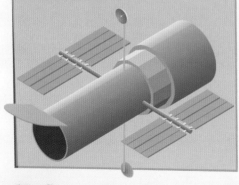

Since their invention in the 1600s, telescopes have grown increasingly bigger and more powerful, yet have always suffered from a problem: Light passing through Earth's atmosphere is distorted, blurring our view of the skies. The atmosphere also blocks out most forms of radiation, except for visible light and radio waves, limiting our understanding of the cosmos. All this changed in 1989 with the launch of one of the first space telescopes, the Cosmic Background Explorer (COBE), sent up to study the faint infrared and microwave radiation from the early universe. For the first time, we were able to see the universe clearly, in all wavelengths of light.

Launched in 1991, Compton was no ordinary telescope: It detected gamma rays, enabling it to track objects such as black holes, quasars, supernovae, and neutron stars.

Fascinating Fact

The Kepler space observatory was launched in 2009 to search for Earthlike planets orbiting other stars. By 2018, it had discovered 2,342 planets, many of them rocky, like Earth. The first rocky planet found at the right distance from its star to allow for life was called Kepler-69c. It's around 2,700 light-years away.

Chandra Space Telescope

Chandra, launched in 1999, is positioned 200 times higher than Hubble, in an elliptical orbit. It is equipped with four pairs of barrel-shaped mirrors that can pick up X-rays from very hot parts of the universe, including exploded stars, colliding galaxies, and matter around black holes.

Spitzer Space Telescope

This telescope, launched in 2003, studies infrared light, which manifests as heat. For this reason, Spitzer's detecting instruments must be kept extremely cold.

A solar shield and a liquid helium tank keep them around 1.4 Kelvin, which is very close to absolute zero, the lowest temperature possible.

Biospheres are self-contained ecosystems built on Earth to simulate an inhabited base on Mars. People can live for long periods in these bases to experience what it'll be like living on another planet.

How Do We Survive in Space?

O ne of the most challenging aspects of crewed space missions is keeping astronauts healthy. Air, food, and water must be provided, and human waste products must be eliminated. Crew members must also be protected from extremes of temperature, pressure, radiation, and micrometeorites. Since the earliest human spaceflights, scientists have worked at developing life support systems (LSS) that keep astronauts comfortable, and monitor their health and the environment of the spacecraft.

Atmosphere

LSS equipment onboard the ISS uses electricity from solar panels to obtain oxygen from water. Filters remove human waste gases from the air. In the future, plants grown in space may provide oxygen and absorb carbon dioxide. Human waste gases could even help provide propulsion for the spacecraft.

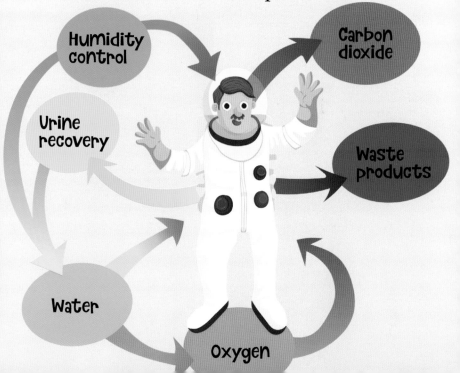

Humidity control

Carbon dioxide

Urine recovery

Waste products

Water

Oxygen

Water

Future space missions may be able to obtain water from the atmosphere or ice deposits on the moons and planets they visit. Today, however, water for drinking, cleaning, and keeping cool must be reclaimed from wastewater. Urine and old bathing water is filtered to remove its impurities and then reused.

I try not to think where this has been!

To shield astronauts from extremes of heat and cold, spacecraft have heat-resistant insulation. Air and water heat exchangers keep the atmosphere onboard cool and dry.

Why It Works

Oxygen can be obtained from water by a process called electrolysis. Each molecule of water contains two hydrogen atoms and an oxygen atom. Running an electric current through water causes these atoms to separate and recombine as the gases hydrogen and oxygen.

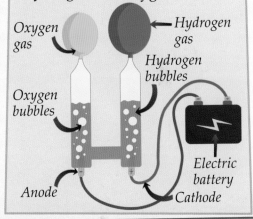

Oxygen gas

Hydrogen gas

Oxygen bubbles

Hydrogen bubbles

Anode

Electric battery

Cathode

Food

Today, crews get their food supplies from Earth. Growing plants in microgravity is difficult, because water spreads evenly in the soil and not enough reaches the roots. If plants could be grown using an artificial gravity system, nutrients obtained from composting toilets could be used to fertilize new crops.

Making fertilizer

Private Spaceflight

Increasingly, private individuals and companies are launching their own space missions. They have developed spaceplanes, rockets, and satellites. Also, there are plans for privately funded space probes, as well as space stations and rocket trips for tourists who wish to be astronauts for a day.

The Moon continues to be a focus of interest for future missions. A base near the Moon's north pole would provide lots of sunlight for solar energy and crop growth.

The Future of Space Travel

Humankind has made huge advances in space exploration since Sputnik, and the future is likely to witness many more exciting moments. We might see a permanent base on the Moon, the first crewed mission to Mars, the mining of asteroids, and the first space tourists. There are challenges: Space is vast, and our fastest probe would take 18,000 years to reach the nearest star. It remains extremely costly to reach space and keep humans alive once they are there. Someday, perhaps there will be new technologies that will make spacefaring more convenient and human-friendly.

Tower to Space

Scientists have speculated that a cheaper way of accessing space would be by building an extremely high tower that reaches beyond Earth's atmosphere by about 60 miles (100 km). Rockets launched from there would need far less fuel. However, the engineering challenges of building anything so high are massive.

Don't look down!

Space Elevator

Another way of reaching space could be a "space elevator," a cable made of some very strong, light material, anchored to Earth's surface and stretching above the level of geosynchronous orbit (22,300 miles or 36,000 km). Vehicles could climb the cable into orbit. Scientists calculate that Earth's rotation would keep the cable taut.

Earth

Elevator

Cable   Space station

Future probes will be able to make decisions on their own, based on data they sense around them, and modify their actions as the situation changes.

Can You Believe It?

Terraforming means changing a planet's environment so it becomes more like Earth, enabling people, plants, and animals to live there. Some scientists think it may be possible to terraform Mars over many decades by adding gases to form an Earthlike atmosphere, which traps heat and warms the planet's surface.

Mars Stage 1   *Mars Stage 2*

Mars Stage 3   *Mars Stage 4*

Glossary

Airlock A compartment with controlled pressure and parallel sets of doors to allow movement in and out of a spacecraft.

Antenna A device by which radio signals are transmitted or received.

Artificial satellite A human-made object placed in orbit around Earth or some other body in space.

Asteroid A small, rocky, or metallic body that orbits a star.

Bends A painful condition in which nitrogen causes bubbles to form in the body.

Black hole An invisible region of space with such an intense gravitational pull that nothing, not even light, can escape from it.

Booster The first stage of a multistage launch vehicle, or a shorter-burning rocket used to add extra thrust to a rocket.

Bus The framework of a spacecraft to which other parts are attached.

Comet A celestial object made up of a core of ice and dust.

Elliptical orbit An orbit that has the shape of an ellipse, or oval.

EVA Stands for extravehicular activity; another word for *space walk*.

Geosynchronous orbit An orbit around Earth in which one revolution is completed in the period it takes Earth to rotate once around its axis.

Gyroscope A device used in automatic navigation systems to provide stability and direction.

Infrared light Light with a wavelength just greater than that of the red end of the visible spectrum.

Lander A spacecraft designed to land on the surface of a celestial body.

Light-year A unit of distance equivalent to the distance that light travels in a year.

Microgravity Very weak gravity, as found in an orbiting spacecraft.

Micrometeorite A microscopic particle in space.

Neutron star A celestial object of very small dimension but very high density.

Payload Equipment, personnel, or satellites carried by a spacecraft.

Probe A spacecraft that carries scientific equipment but no people.

Propellant A substance, such as fuel, that propels something.

Quasar A massive, extremely remote celestial object emitting very large amounts of energy.

Radiation The emission of high-energy particles, which can cause damage to humans.

Rover A remote-controlled vehicle for driving over extraterrestrial terrain.

Solar panel A panel designed to absorb the Sun's rays and convert it into electricity.

Solar system The Sun and all the planets, moons, asteroids, and other bodies in orbit around it.

Spaceplane An aircraft that is capable of traveling into space.

Space station An artificial satellite used as a long-term base for crewed operations in space.

Supernova A star that suddenly increases in brightness because of a huge explosion.

Thrust The propulsive force of a rocket engine.

Transceiver A device that can both transmit and receive communications.

Ultraviolet light Light with a wavelength just shorter than the violet end of the visible spectrum.

Index